IN THE IMAGE OF GOD

GENDER & SEXUAL IDENTITY

Concordia
Publishing House

Founded in 1869 as the publishing arm of The Lutheran Church—Missouri Synod, Concordia Publishing House gives all glory to God for the blessing of 150 years of opportunities to provide resources that are faithful to the Holy Scriptures and the Lutheran Confessions.

3558 S. Jefferson Ave.
St. Louis, MO 63118-3968
1-800-325-3040 • www.cph.org

Manufactured in the United States of America

1 2 3 4 5 6 7 8 9 10 28 27 26 25 24 23 22 21 20 19

HOW CAN THIS WORLD BE SO CONFUSING,

especially when it comes to talking about someone's gender? Aren't you just born male or female? You've probably heard your parent or another adult asking questions just like these. Maybe you've even asked these questions yourself. We'll take a look at these questions and many others in the pages that follow.

In these pages, we're going to talk frankly about gender and sexuality issues. This might make you uncomfortable, but we want to make sure we clearly communicate the issues facing you in the world today and that you really understand these issues. The information we share is rooted in the truth, not fake news, not personal opinion, not feelings. We'll share the truth concerning these issues found in God's Word.

Now these truths aren't necessarily popular, and your friends might not agree with everything it says in this book. At times, you might be upset about what we say and tempted to throw this book across the room. (Go ahead. It's little and lightweight, so it shouldn't break anything.) But we encourage you to pick it up and look again at the truth.

Don't take the words of this book as an excuse to hate someone different from you. Nor should you read that we hate anyone who is wrestling with gender identity and sexuality. Nothing could be further from the truth. Rather, we want to provide you with the tools needed to have open and honest conversations—ones that lead others to understanding the truths found in God's Word.

GOD'S IMAGE

So let's start at the beginning—the beginning of time that is. God has been busy creating light and darkness, planets, plants, and all matter of animals. Now the time has come for His greatest creation—humankind:

> So God created man in His own image, in the image of God He created him; male and female He created them. And God blessed them. And God said to them, "Be fruitful and multiply and fill the earth and subdue it."
>
> (Genesis 1:27–28)

© iStock.com

DID YOU CATCH THAT? God the Father created humankind in two sexes: male and female. Just in case you missed this point, Jesus Himself repeats it in Matthew's Gospel:

> He answered, "Have you not read that He who created them from the beginning made them male and female, and said, 'Therefore a man shall leave his father and his mother and hold fast to his wife, and the two shall become one flesh'?"
> (Matthew 19:4-5)

But it isn't just the Bible that tells us that we are made either male or female. When it comes to this topic, science and the Bible agree.

BODY BASICS

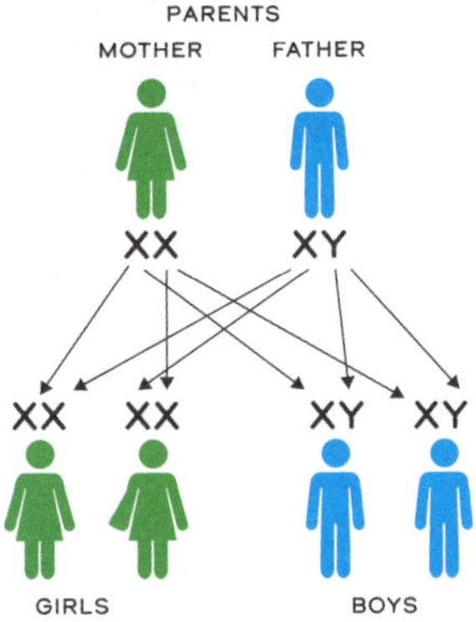

© iStock.com

Every cell in the human body normally contains forty-six chromosomes in twenty-three pairs. One of these pairs determines the sex of the individual. Individuals who have two X chromosomes are female. Those with an X and a Y are male. In other words, every one of the 37.2 trillion cells in your body is genetically programmed as male or female.

In some rare occasions, babies are born with forty-seven chromosomes, a genetic condition involving an extra X chromosome. In males, this XXY pattern is called Klinefelter Syndrome. Seen about once in every 650 births, most men never even realize they have this condition. The female XXX pattern, known as Triple X Syndrome, occurs once in every 1,000 births. For females, symptoms vary from unnoticeable to mild developmental delays and learning disabilities. In both cases, the individual's genitals are underdeveloped and they are unable to conceive.

GENDER OR SEX?

For years when you said someone was male or female, you were talking about both their biological sex and their gender. But nowadays many people in this world confuse or try to separate these two concepts. They would define your biological gender as your "sex." Meanwhile your "gender" is how you choose to express your "maleness" or "femaleness." Some sources trace this shift in meaning back to author D. H. Lawrence in the late 1920s. Another significant influencer to the change in meaning was Supreme Court Justice Ruth Bader Ginsburg, who had her secretary change the wording in legal briefs from "sex discrimination" to "gender discrimination" because she was tired of seeing the word *sex* appearing in so many legal briefs.

GENDER IDENTITY—SEXUAL IDENTITY

Gender identity is considered very personal. It consists of how someone perceives themselves and how they express that perception to the world. This is different from sexual identity, which is who the individual feels sexual attraction toward.

GENDER IDENTITY

A PE teacher in Florida was punished because he refused to supervise a transgender female student (a female identifying as a male) who was allowed to use the boys' locker room. The school district permitted this without informing parents in advance, so some boys were caught literally with their pants down.

The confusing world of gender identity makes everyday life quite confusing. Students as young as elementary school age are claiming a gender identity different from the sex that they were assigned at birth. School districts are scrambling to accommodate students who self-declare their new gender identity. In their efforts to accommodate the few, these new policies infringe on the majority of students. This Florida case is just one example of how the majority of students were inconvenienced in order to accommodate one student.

For many years, the only gender transitions you heard about were among adults. Now children as young as ten years old are undergoing gender transitions. Many begin taking medication to prevent the onset of puberty and the physical changes which would normally occur for someone of their birth sex.

Even with gender reassignment surgery the reality of the person's genetics remains the same. Even with physical changes and medications, they still have either XX or XY chromosomes.

A LOGICAL FALLACY

No standard exists for someone to declare themselves a different gender. It doesn't require screening or an examination by medical or psychological professionals. The person can literally say, "I'm done being a girl; I'm going to be a boy now."

Think about the fallacy in logic here. I could decide I no longer want to be a middle-aged dad. Instead, I'd like to be a twenty-five-year-old surfer dude. How likely is that to happen? NEVER! In the same way, I could decide I'm tired of being a human, that I'd like to be a zebra in the zoo. Just because I decide I want something doesn't mean it's going to happen or that it is real.

PRONOUNS MATTER

In one Southern Illinois community, teachers are no longer allowed to refer to students in their classrooms as "boys and girls." School officials say pupils may only be addressed as "students" or "learners." Failure to comply with this new policy will result in discipline with potential reduction in salary for repeat offenses.

Believe it or not, pronouns matter to someone besides your English teacher. I'm sure you would rather be addressed by name rather than "Hey, you over there."

But those who advocate gender sensitivity take it one step further, going so far as to claim using the unwanted gender pronouns for someone is equivalent to personal assault or violence against that individual. For instance, referring to someone as "he" or "him" when that person identifies as female, or when that person just doesn't want to have any gender labels attached no matter how they identify, is considered an attack.

CONFUSED YET?

Gender advocates suggest that when addressing someone you do not know, you should first ask the individual for their preferred personal pronouns. If in doubt, they say, use gender-inclusive pronouns such as ze (for he or she). Never mind that these words don't exist in most dictionaries but rather have been created to fit the desires of transitioning individuals. Many experts suggest the use of they or their as safe gender-neutral first-person pronouns. Once again, transgender activists are asking you to take part in sinful delusion.

PERSONAL VIOLENCE

Recently a high school French teacher in Virginia was fired for refusing to use male pronouns for a student who transitioned from female to male between ninth and tenth grades. The teacher agreed to use the student's new male name when addressing him in class, but officials claim the teacher's unintentional use of the wrong pronouns for the student represented misgendering and discriminated against the student.

How did we get to this point when people are so offended by words that they consider being called by the unwanted gender pronoun a violent attack on their person?

Schools and governments struggle with regulating speech, but many question if their attempts to restrict so-called hate speech infringes on the First Amendment's freedom-of-speech guarantees.

LEARNING A NEW VOCABULARY

Learning the difference between gender identity and sexual identity also means learning a whole new vocabulary. Gender and sexual identity descriptors are fairly extensive. Some of the most commonly used terms can be found in the glossary at the end of this book.

SEXUAL IDENTITY

Who you are attracted to sexually defines your sexual identity. Someone's sexual identity is quite different from his or her gender identity. This can be especially confusing when someone's gender and sexual identities seemingly conflict. For instance: a person, born male but who gender identifies as female, might be attracted to men but claims to be heterosexual, not homosexual. Confused yet? Yep, me too!

AS YOU PROBABLY KNOW THERE ARE THREE BASIC SEXUAL IDENTITIES.

Heterosexual—attracted to opposite sex. Homosexual—attracted to same sex. Bisexual—attracted to both sexes equally or at different points in life. While there are smaller sub-categories within each of these, we won't take the time to talk about those now.

THE REALITY OF THE WORLD'S PLAN

> Now the works of the flesh are evident: sexual immorality, impurity, sensuality, idolatry, sorcery, enmity, strife, jealousy, fits of anger, rivalries, dissensions,

divisions, envy, drunkenness, orgies, and things like these. I warn you, as I warned you before, that those who do such things will not inherit the kingdom of God.
(Galatians 5:19-21)

OUR WORLD IS A BROKEN PLACE.

The sin brought upon the earth by Adam and Eve has festered and grown for thousands of years. God's plan for sexuality devolved from a perfect relationship between man and woman to a warped sexual landscape of same-sex attractions, individuals changing genders, and worse.

The world's plan for sexuality and gender identity embraces "do what feels good," "express yourself," "live for the moment," and any other number of self-centered philosophies. Humankind's desire to be like God and in charge of their own future hasn't changed since the original sin in the Garden of Eden. If you are the center of your own world, it makes it so much easier to justify your behavior. If there is no God, you only need to worry about yourself, what you want, what makes you feel good.

Some will even say, if there is a god, surely he wants what's best for you. He'll let you work out your issues because he loves you so much. There's no such thing as punishment for sinful behavior in this religion because this god is just too kind and loving.

Sadly, the world's plan is just a path to destruction, a plan to lead you away from the true God to an eternity separated from Him. The world wants you to be happy now, with no concern for the future. It doesn't matter that you suffer for all eternity in hell.

THE REALITY OF GOD'S PLAN

> So God created man in His own image, in the image of God He created him; male and female He created them.
> (Genesis 1:27)

As we look at God's plan for your gender and sexual identity, we need to start in the place where God speaks to us today, His Word. In His creation, God specifically created male and female—man and woman. In Genesis 2, we learn that Adam was created first from the dust of the earth. But when God saw that Adan needed a "helper" for companionship and procreation, He created Eve from Adam's rib. Woman is literally "bone of his bone" and "flesh of his flesh" (Genesis 2:23).

> My frame was not hidden from you, when I was being made in secret, intricately woven in the depths of the earth. Your eyes saw my unformed substance; in your book were written, every one of them, the days that were formed for me, when as yet there was none of them.
>
> (Psalm 139:15-16)

These words from David's psalm remind us that we were known by God even before we were born. Remember how we talked about the genetics that make you male or female? That's what God is talking about in His Word here in the Psalms. He knew that you were going to be a boy or girl even before you were born, while your body was still being formed within your mother's womb.

> He answered, "Have you not read that He who created them from the beginning made them male and female, and said, 'Therefore a man shall leave his father and his mother and hold fast to his wife, and the two shall become one flesh'? So they are no longer two but one

flesh. What therefore God has joined together, let not man separate."

(Matthew 19:4-6)

The next part of God's plan comes from the mouth of Jesus Himself. Here, Jesus reaffirms the creation account that God makes you uniquely male or female. Christ's words also lead you to the next step in God's plan. God intends man and woman to be together in a perfect marriage relationship so connected that they literally become "one flesh." Does this mean you must get married? Of course not! But note the marriage relationship God talks about is between one man and one woman—an unpopular position in today's world, but the only marriage relationship God approves in His Word.

I know, we're hitting you hard with lots of God's directions for marriage and relationships. But we also realize not everyone is interested in marriage. In fact, God addresses this in His Word as well.

The disciples said to Him, "If such is the case of a man with his wife, it is better not to marry." But He said to them, "Not everyone can receive this saying, but only those to whom it is given. For

> there are eunuchs who have been so from birth, and there are eunuchs who have been made eunuchs by men, and there are eunuchs who have made themselves eunuchs for the sake of the kingdom of heaven. Let the one who is able to receive this receive it."
>
> (Matthew 19:10-12)

Not everyone is cut out for marriage. As Jesus addresses this subject for His disciples, He talks about specific groups of eunuchs (those who either cannot or chose not to be sexually active). Some who serve the Lord choose not to marry in order to focus on their ministry, but God does not require celibacy in order to serve Him.

Paul, who remained unmarried throughout his ministry, addresses the challenges in his first letter to the church in Corinth.

> Now concerning the matters about which you wrote: "It is good for a man not to have sexual relations with a woman." But because of the temptation to sexual immorality, each man should have his own wife and each woman her own husband. The husband should give to his wife her

> conjugal rights, and likewise the wife to her husband.
>
> (1 Corinthians 7:1-3)

In this letter, Paul repeats God's plan for marriage between one man and one woman who remain sexually pure and committed to each other. Interestingly, part of remaining sexually pure includes not denying sex to one's spouse.

God created you with a sex drive. It's a perfectly natural inclination, but one designed only for use within the marriage relationship. The world wants you to act on your sexual desires, yet God directs us to refrain from sex outside of marriage. (See 1 Thessalonians 4:3–6.)

> Now as a concession, not a command, I say this. I wish that all were as I myself am. But each has his own gift from God, one of one kind and one of another. To the unmarried and the widows I say that it is good for them to remain single, as I am. But if they cannot exercise self-control, they should marry. For it is better to marry than to burn with passion.
>
> (1 Corinthians 7:6-9)

Paul tells his readers that some have a gift that allows them to remain single and sexually pure. This gift allows men and women like Paul to focus on their mission and ministry. If you can't control your sexual urges, then Paul encourages you to marry rather than live in sin.

God's plan for your gender identity and sexual identity stands in opposition to the world's plan. God has a standard for you designed to set you apart from the rest of the world. God knows we are unable to live out His plan perfectly so He gave us His own Son, Jesus, as our Savior from sin.

RESPONDING TO THE ISSUES

Since the world stands in opposition to God's plan, Christians face challenges when responding to the issues surrounding gender and sexuality. Every situation is unique, but all share the need for a generous application of grace as you seek to clearly communicate God's Word concerning this topic.

AT HOME

Many families have already been confronted with the reality of gender or sexual identity. If it hasn't happened in your family yet, you can be thankful to God. At the same time, you should prepare yourself for how you might deal with a family member who suddenly announces their new gender or sexual identity.

THE FIRST STEP IS NOT TO OVERREACT.

Often the person making the announcement has struggled with making their perceived identity known to family members. They may be feeling extreme anxiety or even fear of rejection when sharing this news. You need to remember the relationship you already have with this person when they are sharing their struggle.

Sadly, some people will avoid telling you about their struggles with gender and/or sexual identity because of your Christian faith. They assume that your first reaction will be one of judgment, rather than one of caring. In these situations, It's important to remember the difference between condemning the sin and condemning the sinner. God calls us to condemn sin, but it is not our job to pass judgment on the sinner.

Work to maintain your relationship with the individual as you guide them to what God's Word says about sin, especially sexual sins. It's important that they understand that we are all sinful and equally forgiven by the blood of Jesus, which was shed for all believers. As they receive forgiveness, help them to understand that part of repentance means turning away from their sin and toward God's plan for their lives with the help of the Holy Spirit.

Help connect your family member to a trusted adult leader in your congregation. This could include your pastor, DCE, deaconess, or other church leader. These individuals should be able to guide your family member to appropriate counseling and other resources as needed.

Finally, pray! Pray for your relationship with the person. Pray that God would work through His Word and Spirit to show the person the true answers to their struggles found only in Him.

AT SCHOOL

The average middle school through high school in our country today is a complex microcosm of society in general. Then throw in some raging hormones, puberty, and textbooks just to keep things interesting. Many teens feel out of place at school, and having doubts about your sexual identity or gender only adds to the confusion. Teens are quick to judge anyone they perceive as "different"

—anyone who does not match their preconceived notions of what "normal" looks like in that school.

When a close friend comes to you with news concerning their sexual or gender identity, the first and most important thing you can do is protect that information. The temptation to share their struggle publicly will be great. But I strongly urge you to honor your friend's privacy unless they've told you otherwise.

Like the family member, make sure your friend gets support from a trusted counselor, pastor, or other professional. Walk alongside your friend as they navigate the path of discovering who God really intends them to be.

AT CHURCH

Well-intentioned church members may only cause further harm when dealing with issues of sexual or gender identity. The church has often struggled when dealing with sexual sins, and these issues are no different. When hearing of a member's struggle with gender identity or sexuality, you often hear two distinct reactions: judging and rejecting the individual as a hopeless sinner, or trying to "fix" the person by "praying it out of them."

Both of these reactions are recipes for disaster. The outright rejection of the sinner denies them the Gospel forgiveness and the opportunity to repent of their sin and turn away from it. In the same way, trying to "fix" the sinner works just about as well as trying to fix our own sins.

Working through the complex issues surrounding gender and sexuality takes time and the care of a sensitive church professional, such as a pastor, DCE, or deaconess, who may also use the services of a Christian counselor or therapist when working with individuals struggling with their sexual identity.

ON CAMPUS

Public universities are frequently in the forefront of widespread acceptance for sexual identity and gender issues. The open exchange of information and outright encouragement of sexual freedom and gender exploration can be confusing for Christian students who hold firmly to the biblical standard for marriage and sexuality.

Christians students may not be allowed to share their viewpoints, or they could even fear reprisal from campus groups that advocate more liberal sexual practices. The open expression of ideas on college and university campuses seems to apply to everyone, except Christians.

In some cases, the suppression of expression has become so severe that Christian students feel unsafe and their First Amendment rights to free speech have been violated.

Swedish university professor Germund Hesslow came under attack in late 2018. A specialist in neurophysiology at Lund University, Hesslow cited research supporting the idea that differences between men and women are biologically founded, and as such genders cannot be simply social constructs. Following his lecture, students complained to university officials, who then attempted to force Hesslow to renounce his statements.

Some colleges and universities have a much more balanced approach. A Christian college professor recently shared information about a graduate foundations of education class she taught. We'll let her tell her own story:

Through class readings and discussions, it became clear the students of my class were interested in learning more about transgender students in our pre-K–12 schools. This was not a topic I was jumping to tackle, but I decided to do some research and give it a try.

I assigned my students to read their text or a relevant article each week. They were asked to reflect on the reading and write a two-page paper about their thoughts. They were given free rein in their writing. I would collect the papers before class and read them. I would sculpt the conversation and objectives into our discussions based on the papers' contents. Reading students' thoughts gave me a head start into knowing their perspectives and the potential conversations.

The students in my class had opinions about transgender people that were across the board. There were strong feelings about transgender students being just like anyone else and who should have the same rights as everyone. There were also students who felt that identifying as transgender was not natural and went against God's will for the world. They felt strongly that their beliefs mirrored science. You were born male or female and that is what you are.

My biggest concern was that either side would have a difficult time understanding the point of view of the other side. My class previously focused on the humanity of all people, in regards to race and exceptionality. We have drawn heavily on the idea that as people it is our responsibility to treat others as human beings first. I was hoping to draw upon this idea throughout our class.

I began the class with basic information from the National Center for Transgender Equality. I wanted to give the class a framework for the language used to discuss this issue. I also wanted to present a human side. I showed several videos of people who have transitioned. Finally, I included a discussion concerning our responsibility as educators to follow the law of our state and communities.

Students were eager to discuss the information, videos, and their future as teachers. I was happy to see that the individuals on both sides of the issue felt comfortable and safe in our classroom to share their perspectives. At one point, a person who was not in favor of transgender laws said something that another student was somewhat shocked by. I remember needing to interrupt and encourage those students to remember that their classmates are humans and also have a point of view that is worthy of being heard.

By the end of the conversation, all of my students were thankful that we had this discussion.

WHERE TO TURN

The newest version of Luther's Small Catechism with Explanation addresses the issue of gender and sexuality:

What is the Christian perspective on persons who are confused about their sexual identity?

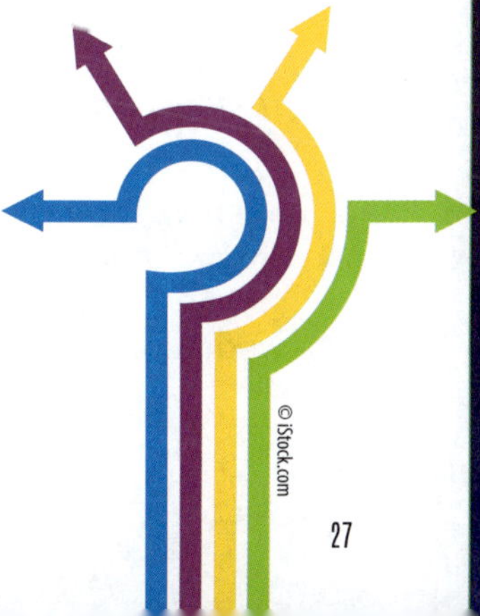

During adolescence, most people come to realize a growing interest and attraction toward the opposite sex—a desire and attraction that God intended when He created us male and female and established marriage between man and woman. Christians realize that a desire and attraction for the opposite sex is the God-given basis for marriage, for the conception and birth of children, and for the future of earthly human life.

Some persons, however, may discover that they are attracted to individuals of the same sex. Others may feel uncomfortable with the sex they were born with and wish they were, or believe they are, the opposite sex with the wrong body. Such desires result from our fallen nature and are contrary to the will of God. Therefore we should

A. *remember that our chief identity is given in Baptism—that we are God's children and heirs of heaven;*

B. *respect our identity as male or female as indicated by the body God gave us;*

C. *respect God's intentions for us as male and female;*

D. *remember and be obedient to God's command that all desires for sexual activity are to be curbed and disciplined until we are married;*

E. *remember that while most people will marry, God's Word also praises and blesses those who serve Him by living chastely without marrying;*

F. *seek the assistance of parents and also pastors, counselors, or other Christian professionals where that is needed or beneficial;*

G. **trust that God's grace is sufficient for us, and look to Christ for daily forgiveness, strength, and contentment.**

WHAT'S NEXT?

The world of gender and sexual identity remains a confusing place filled with those who would encourage Christian young people to compromise their beliefs while giving in to the world's standards. As Christians, we have the obligation to speak the truth in love to those around us, especially those who fall prey to the devil's schemes. As you live out your lives, I pray that you spend time in God's Word as His Spirit works in you to strengthen your faith as you witness the truth of God's Word to a fallen world.

A GLOSSARY OF GENDER & SEXUAL IDENTITY TERMS

agender: gender identity that doesn't align with male or female; also known as gender neutral.

androgynous: not distinctly masculine or feminine.

binary: a viewpoint that gender is solely male or female, man and woman.

bisexual: a person sexually attracted to both men and women.

cisgender: describes someone whose gender identity matches their birth sex.

gay: term generally used for male homosexuals.

gender dysphoria: the clinical term for someone whose birth gender does not match the gender with which they identify.

gender expression: the external appearance of the person's gender identity.

gender fluid: a person who does not identify as a single gender.

gender identity: the innermost concept of self as man, woman, or some blend of both.

gender nonconforming: refers to people who behave in a way that does not conform to traditional gender roles.

gender questioning: someone who is actively exploring how to express their gender identity.

genderqueer: someone who rejects standard categories of gender expression; they see themselves as both male and female.

heterosexual: a person primarily attracted to members of the opposite sex.

homophobia: an irrational fear of homosexuals.

homosexual: a person primarily attracted to members of the same sex.

lesbian: a general term for female homosexuals.

misgender: addressing someone using words and pronouns that don't correctly reflect the identity with which they identify.

nonbinary: any gender that falls outside of the binary system.

pronouns: nongender specific pronouns include *hir* to replace *him* and *her* as well as *s/he* or *ze* to replace *he* and *she*.

queer: an umbrella term used by people to express fluid identities and orientations.

sex: the gender assigned at child at birth,

typically based on their external anatomy.
sexual orientation: distinct preference for partners of a particular sex.
straight: a term used by homosexuals for heterosexuals.
transgender: a general term for people whose gender identity and expression is different from their gender assigned at birth.
transitioning: the medical and social process through which someone goes when moving from one gender to another.
transsexual person: a term for people who have a gender identity that is different from the sex assigned to them at birth; this term has fallen out of favor.